THIS BOOK BELONGS TO

D1713674

Christmas Memories

Would you rather

open presents one by one

or

all at once?

Would you rather

have a Christmas tree made of candy canes

or

gingerbread?

Would you rather

wear a Christmas sweater that sings

or

lights up?

Would you rather

get only socks

or

only hats for Christmas?

Would you rather

unwrap a gift slowly

or

rip the paper off quickly?

Would you rather

have snow that smells like cookies

or

hot cocoa?

Would you rather

have your house decorated with too many lights

or

too many ornaments?

Would you rather

hear the same Christmas song on repeat

or

watch the same Christmas movie over and over?

Would you rather

eat Christmas dinner with no dessert

or

just have dessert?

Would you rather

help Santa deliver presents

or

help the elves make toys?

Would you rather

have Christmas dinner every night

or

never again?

Would you rather

receive a gift you don't want

or

no gift at all?

Would you rather

have your Christmas tree decorated
only in red

or

only in green?

Would you rather

wear Christmas pajamas

or

an ugly Christmas sweater all day?

Would you rather

have Christmas lights that blink

or

that stay on all the time?

Would you rather

get one giant present

or

a bunch of small ones?

Would you rather

make a snow angel

or

build a snow fort?

Would you rather

receive only homemade gifts

or

only store-bought gifts?

Would you rather

have to untangle Christmas lights

or

wrap all the presents?

Would you rather

have a white Christmas every year

or

only once in a lifetime?

Would you rather

have a Christmas party with just your family

or

with all your friends?

Would you rather

find a hidden present under the tree

or

an extra stocking filled with candy?

Would you rather

have Christmas music playing all day

or

Christmas movies on TV all day?

Would you rather

eat Christmas cookies every day

or

Christmas candy?

Would you rather

get to open one present early

or

get to stay up late on Christmas Eve?

Would you rather

have a Christmas tree that's too tall

or

too short?

Would you rather

get to ride in Santa's sleigh

or

drive it?

Would you rather

get a Christmas card from a snowman

or

from a reindeer?

Would you rather

drink hot cocoa with marshmallows

or

without?

Would you rather

have your house smell like gingerbread

or

peppermint?

Christmas Carols

Would you rather

sing like an elf

or

a reindeer?

Would you rather

hum "Jingle Bells"

or

"Deck the Halls" all day?

Would you rather

sing "Frosty the Snowman" with a carrot nose

or

"Rudolph" with a red nose?

Would you rather

sing "Silent Night" loudly

or

"Joy to the World" quietly?

Would you rather

sing "Jingle Bells" slowly

or

"Deck the Halls" quickly?

Would you rather

sing "Jingle Bell Rock" while dancing

or

jumping?

Would you rather

sing "Frosty" with snow falling

or

"Let It Snow" in the rain?

Would you rather

hum "Jingle Bells" while brushing your teeth

or

"O Holy Night" while washing hands?

Would you rather

sing "Rudolph" in pajamas

or

"Santa Claus is Coming" in a hat?

Would you rather

sing "Jingle Bells" with jingling shoes

or

"Up on the Housetop" with a drum?

Would you rather

sing "Deck the Halls" with a candy cane

or

"Jingle Bell Rock" with a guitar?

Would you rather

sing "O Christmas Tree" in a tree costume

or

"Winter Wonderland" ice skating?

Would you rather

sing "We Three Kings" with toys

or

"Drummer Boy" with pots?

Would you rather

sing "Santa Claus is Coming" in a whisper

or

"Frosty" like a robot?

Would you rather

sing "Jingle Bells" backwards

or

"Silent Night" with closed eyes?

Would you rather

sing "12 Days of Christmas" with friends

or

"Jingle Bell Rock" with toys?

Would you rather

sing "Frosty" with a snowball

or

"Rudolph" with antlers?

Would you rather

sing "O Christmas Tree" with a pine cone

or

"Winter Wonderland" with a snowflake?

Would you rather

sing "Silent Night" with a stuffed toy

or

"Joy to the World" with a ball?

Would you rather

sing "Jingle Bells" with shoes

or

"We Wish You" with a hat?

Would you rather

sing "Drummer Boy" on a table

or

"Santa Claus" tiptoeing?

Would you rather

sing "O Holy Night" with a star

or

"Frosty" with a nose?

Would you rather

sing "Joy to the World" spinning

or

"Jingle Bells" clapping?

Would you rather

sing "Jingle Bell Rock" jumping

or

"Deck the Halls" waving?

Would you rather

sing "We Three Kings" with a crown

or

"Drummer Boy" with a stick?

Would you rather

sing "O Christmas Tree" with an ornament

or

"Winter Wonderland" with a snowball?

Would you rather

sing "Jingle Bells" with a bell shirt

or

"Santa Claus" with a hat?

Would you rather

sing "Silent Night" with a candle

or

"Joy to the World" with a star?

Would you rather

sing "Rudolph" with a red nose

or

"Frosty" with a snowflake?

Would you rather

sing "We Wish You" eating a candy cane

or

"Silent Night" sipping cocoa?

Christmas Eve Traditions

Would you rather

hang stockings with your feet

or

decorate the tree with your elbows?

Would you rather

help Santa pack his sleigh

or

help the elves make toys?

Would you rather

open one present early

or

stay up late to see Santa?

Would you rather

have reindeer cookies

or

Santa-shaped pancakes for Christmas Eve dinner?

Would you rather

wrap gifts with sticky tape

or

tie them with spaghetti?

Would you rather

wear a Santa hat all day

or

wear elf shoes that jingle?

Would you rather

have a snowball fight with your family

or

build a snowman?

Would you rather

have hot chocolate with candy canes

or

with marshmallows?

Would you rather

put out carrots for the reindeer

or

cookies for Santa?

Would you rather

hear Santa sing

or

watch the reindeer dance?

Would you rather

decorate the Christmas tree with candy canes

or

with popcorn?

Would you rather

wear Christmas pajamas all day

or

a Christmas sweater?

Would you rather

help hang Christmas lights

or

help bake Christmas cookies?

Would you rather

get a letter from Santa

or

a call from Rudolph?

Would you rather

see a snowstorm

or

Christmas Eve or a rainbow?

Would you rather

have your Christmas dinner in the North Pole

or

in Santa's workshop?

Would you rather

listen to Christmas carols sung by penguins

or

by reindeer?

Would you rather

help make a gingerbread house

or

help make a snow fort?

Would you rather

decorate cookies with frosting

or

with sprinkles?

Would you rather

get a big hug from Santa

or

a high five from an elf?

Would you rather

ride in Santa's sleigh

or

ride on a reindeer?

Would you rather

have Christmas lights that change colors

or

play music?

Would you rather

eat a candy cane that tastes like chocolate

or

a cookie that tastes like peppermint?

Would you rather

help wrap presents with giant bows

or

with sparkly ribbons?

Would you rather

eave Santa a plate of cookies

or

a slice of pie?

Would you rather

have your house covered in Christmas lights

or

snowflakes?

Would you rather

have snowflakes that taste like sugar

or

candy canes that glow in the dark?

Would you rather

help Santa load the sleigh

or

help him steer it?

Would you rather

have a snow globe that sings

or

a Christmas ornament that lights up?

Would you rather

help pack Santa's toy bag

or

help polish Rudolph's nose?

Christmas Crafts

Would you rather

make a Christmas tree out of candy canes

or

out of popcorn?

Would you rather

decorate a gingerbread house with gummy bears

or

with marshmallows?

Would you rather

paint a snowman with pudding

or

with chocolate sauce?

Would you rather

make Christmas ornaments out of pasta

or

out of buttons?

Would you rather

wrap presents with newspaper

or

with toilet paper?

Would you rather

make a wreath out of cookies

or

out of donuts?

Would you rather

build a snowman using cotton balls

or

using marshmallows?

Would you rather

make a Christmas card using glitter

or

using stickers?

Would you rather

create a Christmas stocking out of paper

or

out of old socks?

Would you rather

make a Christmas tree topper out of a starfish

or

out of a teddy bear?

Would you rather

glue candy canes together to make a reindeer

or

to make a sleigh?

Would you rather

create a Christmas ornament using paint

or

using markers?

Would you rather

make a snow globe using glitter

or

using sand?

Would you rather

build a gingerbread house with chocolate

or

with peanut butter?

Would you rather

create a Christmas crown out of wrapping paper

or

out of ribbons?

Would you rather

decorate a Christmas sweater with pom-poms

or

with jingle bells?

Would you rather

paint a Christmas tree with your fingers

or

with a brush?

Would you rather

make a snowflake out of paper

or

out of cotton?

Would you rather

make a Santa hat out of felt

or

out of construction paper?

Would you rather

decorate a Christmas present with bows

or

with stickers?

Would you rather

build a mini snowman inside a jar

or

on a plate?

Would you rather

make Christmas ornaments using play dough

or

using clay?

Would you rather

create a Christmas necklace out of beads

or

out of popcorn?

Would you rather

make a reindeer out of pipe cleaners

or

out of sticks?

Would you rather

decorate a Christmas card with stamps

or

with drawings?

Would you rather

make a snowman ornament out of cotton balls

or

out of marshmallows?

Would you rather

create a Christmas tree out of construction paper

or

out of cardboard?

Would you rather

decorate a gingerbread cookie to look like Santa

or

like a reindeer?

Would you rather

make a Christmas decoration out of recycled materials

or

out of food?

Would you rather

create a holiday wreath out of leaves

or

out of flowers?

Holiday Shopping

Would you rather

shop for toys with a shopping cart that squeaks

or

a shopping cart that wobbles?

Would you rather

buy a giant teddy bear

or

a tiny robot?

Would you rather

have all your presents wrapped in newspaper

or

in banana peels?

Would you rather

shop for holiday treats with sticky fingers

or

with mittens on?

Would you rather

get a gift that makes silly noises

or

a gift that lights up in rainbow colors?

Would you rather

buy a toy that dances

or

a toy that sings?

Would you rather

go shopping in a store filled with candy

or

a store filled with balloons?

Would you rather

have a shopping bag that keeps
falling over

or

one that keeps making funny sounds?

Would you rather

buy a book that tells jokes

or

a book that tells stories?

Would you rather

get a gift wrapped in chocolate

or

wrapped in cotton candy?

Would you rather

shop for gifts with a reindeer

or

with a snowman?

Would you rather

get a toy that can fly

or

a toy that can swim?

Would you rather

buy a pair of shoes that squeak

or

a hat that jingles?

Would you rather

have all your presents come in one big box

or

in many tiny boxes?

Would you rather

shop for gifts with a talking parrot

or

a friendly dog?

Would you rather

buy a toy that can talk

or

a toy that can walk?

Would you rather

wrap gifts using spaghetti noodles

or

with leaves?

Would you rather

shop for presents while riding a skateboard

or

hopping on one foot?

Would you rather

buy a toy car that can shrink

or

a doll that can grow?

Would you rather

have a shopping cart that's too big

or

one that's too small?

Would you rather

buy a toy that glows in the dark

or

a toy that changes colors?

Would you rather

get a gift that's covered in glitter

or

a gift that's covered in stickers?

Would you rather

have a gift that smells like chocolate

or

one that smells like strawberries?

Would you rather

buy a giant candy cane

or

a tiny gingerbread house?

Would you rather

shop for gifts in a store that's freezing cold

or

one that's super warm?

Would you rather

get a toy that can bounce super high

or

a toy that can roll super fast?

Would you rather

get a gift that's wrapped in bubble wrap

or

wrapped in feathers?

Would you rather

buy a stuffed animal that's as big as you

or

one that fits in your pocket?

Would you rather

have a gift that plays music every time
you open it

or

one that dances?

Would you rather

buy a toy that makes animal sounds

or

one that makes robot noises?

Reindeer and Sleigh

Would you rather
have a red nose like Rudolph

or

antlers like a reindeer?

Would you rather
pull Santa's sleigh

or

decorate it with colorful lights?

Would you rather
eat Christmas cookies with Santa

or

share carrots with the reindeer?

Would you rather

have a reindeer as a pet

or

have a sleigh that can fly?

Would you rather

help wrap presents

or

help pack Santa's sleigh?

Would you rather

guide Santa's sleigh through a snowstorm

or

through the starry night sky?

Would you rather
ride a sleigh that plays music

or

one that sparkles with lights?

Would you rather
be best friends with a reindeer

or

an elf?

Would you rather
have reindeer ears

or

a fluffy reindeer tail?

Would you rather

help Santa get ready for his sleigh ride

or

help the reindeer get ready?

Would you rather

have a sleigh made of candy

or

one made of snow?

Would you rather

see the world from a flying sleigh

or

from a reindeer's back?

Would you rather

wear reindeer antlers

or

a Santa hat all day?

Would you rather

take care of Santa's reindeer

or

help load his sleigh?

Would you rather

have a magic sleigh that never needs reindeer

or

have reindeer that can run super fast?

Would you rather

ride in a sleigh pulled by reindeer

or

one pulled by friendly polar bears?

Would you rather

have a reindeer that can talk

or

a sleigh that can sing?

Would you rather

help Santa fly the sleigh

or

help the reindeer navigate?

Would you rather

have a sleigh that can go underwater

or

one that can go through mountains?

Would you rather

fly Santa's sleigh at night

or

during the day?

Would you rather

decorate the reindeer with tinsel

or

with jingle bells?

Would you rather

have a sleigh that changes colors

or

one that makes snowflakes fall?

Would you rather

give a reindeer a bath

or

polish Santa's sleigh?

Would you rather

see the Northern Lights from a sleigh

or

from a reindeer's back?

Would you rather

have a reindeer that can dance

or

a sleigh that can do tricks?

Would you rather

have a sleigh that smells like peppermint

or

one that smells like gingerbread?

Would you rather

ride in a sleigh that goes super fast

or

one that goes super high?

Would you rather

have a reindeer that can jump over houses

or

one that can run on water?

Would you rather

wear a reindeer costume

or

a Santa costume for a day?

Would you rather

have a sleigh that plays your favorite songs

or

one that tells stories?

Santa Claus

Would you rather

ride in Santa's sleigh

or

help Santa wrap presents?

Would you rather

have a beard made of candy canes

or

hair that looks like Christmas lights?

Would you rather

wear Santa's red suit

or

his big black boots?

Would you rather

help the elves make toys

or

help the reindeer practice flying?

Would you rather

have a nose that glows like Rudolph

or

big jingly bells on your ears?

Would you rather

eat Santa's cookies

or

drink his milk?

Would you rather

be able to fly like Santa's reindeer

or

go down chimneys like Santa?

Would you rather

live in Santa's workshop

or

in a giant gingerbread house?

Would you rather

ride on a reindeer

or

on a flying sleigh?

Would you rather

have a snowball fight with Santa

or

build a snowman with him?

Would you rather

have a stocking full of toys

or

a stocking full of candy?

Would you rather

help Santa check his naughty

or

nice list or help the elves make toys?

Would you rather

get to see Santa's toy factory

or

visit the North Pole?

Would you rather

be one of Santa's elves

or

one of his reindeer?

Would you rather

eat candy canes all day

or

eat gingerbread cookies all day?

Would you rather

have Santa's magic powers

or

be able to talk to reindeer?

Would you rather

have a hat like Santa's

or

a scarf like Mrs. Claus?

Would you rather

give Santa a hug

or

give Rudolph a pat?

Would you rather

help decorate Santa's sleigh

or

help decorate his Christmas tree?

Would you rather

go ice skating with Santa

or

go sledding with the elves?

Would you rather

have a magical snow globe

or

a magical Christmas ornament?

Would you rather

help Santa deliver presents

or

help him read letters from kids?

Would you rather

get a present from Santa every day in December

or

one giant present on Christmas Day?

Would you rather

have Santa's laugh (Ho Ho Ho!)

or

Rudolph's red nose?

Would you rather

make toys with the elves

or

make cookies with Mrs. Claus?

Would you rather

visit Santa's reindeer stables

or

his toy workshop?

Would you rather

receive a toy train

or

a toy airplane from Santa?

Would you rather

have a Santa hat that grows when you laugh

or

a scarf that jingles when you walk?

Would you rather

eat Mrs. Claus' special cookies

or

drink her hot chocolate?

Would you rather

ride on a giant candy cane

or

on a big Christmas ornament?

Snow and Winter Activities

Would you rather

build a snowman with a carrot nose

or

a snow dog with a cookie nose?

Would you rather

have a snowball fight with marshmallows

or

with soft pillows?

Would you rather

ice skate on a frozen pond

or

slide down a snowy hill?

Would you rather

drink hot chocolate with extra marshmallows

or

warm apple cider with a cinnamon stick?

Would you rather

make snow angels in a blizzard

or

catch snowflakes on your tongue?

Would you rather

wear a hat made of snow

or

mittens made of ice?

Would you rather

ride a reindeer through the snow

or

a snowmobile that plays music?

Would you rather

go sledding with a penguin

or

skiing with a polar bear?

Would you rather

have a snowball that never melts

or

a snowman that never melts?

Would you rather

wear a snow jacket that sings

or

snow boots that dance?

Would you rather

build an igloo to live in

or

a snow castle to play in?

Would you rather

have snow that tastes like cotton candy

or

snow that glows in the dark?

Would you rather

have snowflakes that giggle when they land

or

snowflakes that sing when they melt?

Would you rather

find a snow-covered treasure chest

or

a snow-covered candy shop?

Would you rather

have a snowball that turns into

or

snow puppy or a snow kitten?

Would you rather

catch a snowflake that grants wishes

or

find a snowball that never stops bouncing?

Would you rather

go on a sleigh ride with Santa

or

build a snow fort with the elves?

Would you rather

have a scarf that grows longer in the snow

or

gloves that change colors in the cold?

Would you rather

make a snowman that talks

or

a snow dog that barks?

Would you rather

walk in snow that makes funny sounds

or

snow that lights up when you step on it?

Would you rather

ride down a snowy hill on a sled

or

on a giant snowflake?

Would you rather

build a snow family with snow animals

or

snow superheroes?

Would you rather

eat a snow cone made of snow

or

a snow cake made of ice?

Would you rather

have a snowball that giggles when thrown

or

a snowflake that dances in the air?

Would you rather

have a snow hat that keeps your
head warm

or

snow shoes that keep your feet warm?

Would you rather

have a snow day every week

or

a snow party every weekend?

Would you rather

catch a snowflake that makes you laugh

or

a snowball that tells jokes?

Would you rather

have a snow fort that's invisible

or

a snowball that never misses?

Would you rather

make a snowman with a snow dog

or

a snowman with a snow cat?

Would you rather

have a snowflake that changes color

or

a snowball that makes music?

Christmas
Tree
Decorations

Would you rather

decorate the Christmas tree with candy canes

or

chocolate bars?

Would you rather

have a tree made of cotton candy

or

a tree made of marshmallows?

Would you rather

hang socks

or

mittens as ornaments on the tree?

Would you rather
put popcorn

or

jellybeans on the tree as a garland?

Would you rather
have blinking lights

or

lights that change colors on your tree?

Would you rather
hang tiny presents

or

tiny snowmen on the tree?

Would you rather

have a star that sings

or

an angel that dances on top of the tree?

Would you rather

decorate the tree with toy cars

or

toy animals?

Would you rather

use ribbons

or

shoelaces to decorate the tree?

Would you rather

have a tree that smells like peppermint

or

a tree that smells like hot chocolate?

Would you rather

hang jingle bells

or

rubber ducks on the tree?

Would you rather

put on a tree topper that spins

or

one that lights up?

Would you rather

have a Christmas tree that's as tall
as a giant

or

as small as a mouse?

Would you rather

decorate the tree with balloons

or

bubbles?

Would you rather

have a tree covered in glitter

or

a tree covered in snowflakes?

Would you rather

hang colorful feathers

or

fuzzy pom-poms on the tree?

Would you rather

have a tree made of candy canes

or

a tree made of gingerbread?

Would you rather

hang shiny spoons

or

shiny coins on the tree?

Would you rather

have a tree that glows in the dark

or

a tree that sings when you clap?

Would you rather

decorate the tree with rainbow colors

or

just two colors, red and green?

Would you rather

have a tree that smells like cinnamon

or

a tree that smells like vanilla?

Would you rather

hang tiny teddy bears

or

tiny robots on the tree?

Would you rather

use spaghetti

or

shoelaces as tinsel on the tree?

Would you rather

have a tree that's always cold

or

a tree that's always warm?

Would you rather

decorate the tree with seashells

or

with snowflakes?

Would you rather

hang mini stockings

or

mini hats on the tree?

Would you rather

have a tree with branches made of candy

or

branches made of cotton?

Would you rather

have a tree that plays music

or

a tree that tells jokes?

Would you rather

hang glittery stars

or

shiny moons on the tree?

Would you rather

have a tree that's all one color

or

a tree that's every color?

Would you rather

wear a Santa hat until New Year's

or

elf shoes with bells?

Would you rather

hang glittery stars

or

shiny moons on the tree?

Would you rather

have a tree that's all one color

or

a tree that's every color?

Made in the USA
Monee, IL
07 December 2024

72730493R00056